I0639414

Thomas Boundy

Liberty's Martyr

A Poem in Eight Cantos. First Edition

Thomas Boundy

Liberty's Martyr
A Poem in Eight Cantos. First Edition

ISBN/EAN: 9783744666008

Printed in Europe, USA, Canada, Australia, Japan

Cover: Foto ©Thomas Meinert / pixelio.de

More available books at **www.hansebooks.com**

THOMAS BOUNDY.

LIBERTY'S MARTYR

A POEM

In Eight Cantos,

BY

THOMAS BOUNDY.

Illustrated.

'Tis to the man and the man's honest worth
　The nation's loyalty in tears upsprings.
Through him the soil of labor shines henceforth
　High o'er the silken broideries of kings.
Born of the people, well he knew to grasp
　The wants and wishes of the weak and small;
Therefore we hold him with no shadowy clasp;
　Therefore his name is household to us all.
　　　　　　　　—Alice Cary.

First Edition.

JERMYN, PA.
THE PRESS PRINTING OFFICE.
1897.

Synopsis.

Canto 1.—A slave auction in New Orleans. One of the slaves sees in a vision Justice with her flashing sword, the future president and bondmen's friend, as well as the principal events of the war. Her vision rudely ended, she hears that memorable utterance, "If ever I get a chance to hit that thing I'll hit it hard." She turns and recognizes the speaker as the central figure of her vision, Abraham Lincoln.

Canto 2.—The events immediately preceding and surrounding Lincoln's inauguration. The substance of his inaugural address.

Canto 3.—The task the new president undertook. The storming of Fort Sumter.

Canto 4.—The battle of Bull Run. "Stonewall" Jackson's bravery and how it turned the tide of battle. Lincoln's calmness and cool judgment under disaster.

ABRAHAM LINCOLN.

From a photograph owned by Mr. Noah Brooks and reproduced here by his permission.

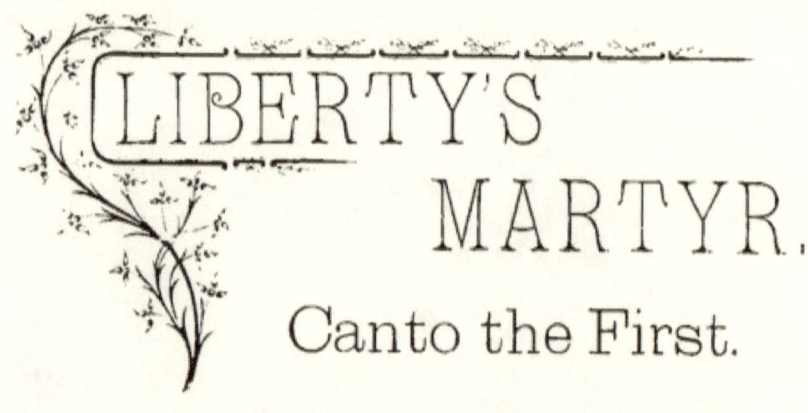

LIBERTY'S MARTYR.

Canto the First.

Abraham Lincoln at a Slave Auction.

'TWAS in a city 'neath a southern sky,
  Where Mississippi rolls in grandeur by;
  A city fanned by breezes from the sea,
Where graceful naiads may have wandered free;
To which Narcissus might with eager stride
Have sped to stand its glassy pools beside —
Observant not that all around was fair
As his resplendent form reflected there —
And lay his form ethereal down to rest,
To pine and die on nature's healthful breast;

A city which the fair Euphrosyne,
The gods of beauty and of harmony,
Might have selected for their festive hall,
But for the blight that held a race in thrall.

An open mart, a miscellaneous crowd,
An auctioneer whose voice was harsh and loud;
His wares were human bodies, and the first
A splendid sample of the race accursed.
He stepped upon a block and faced the throng,
A man of muscle, massive, lithe and strong;
No common frame was his, those limbs of oak
Could slay a common mortal at a stroke.
And yet he meekly stood and heard his price
Leap from small sums to thousands in a trice.
The hammer fell; and thus for sordid gold
A man unto his fellow man was sold.

He stepped aside, a youngster took his place —
The strong man's son—a boy with chubby face
And laughing eyes.   But see! a tearful cloud
Dimmed them the moment that he faced the crowd;
Confused, he gazed, then sought his mother's face,

And the next moment rushed to her embrace.
O, cruel laugh!   O, worse than cruel heart!
Their ruthless owner tore the twain apart.
He never dreamed that e'en a seraph might
Have gazed with rapture on that lovely sight;
He wanted dollars, and for dollars then
He placed the youngster on the block again,
And sold him, too, that child of tender years,
A quivering little mass of sobs and tears.

 Next came the mother.— How her bosom
  heaved!—
Of husband now and baby, too, bereaved,
She stood a victim of the nation's sin;
Her wandering sense heard not the buyers' din;
Her one request, enforced with suppliant tone
And streaming tears, moved not their hearts of
  stone.
Yet all she asked was but the paltry joy
To serve the planter who had bought her boy.
Again the hammer fell; she raised her eyes,
Glanced at her buyer, then upward to the skies

She sent a mute appeal.   An angel there
Marked well the fervor of that silent prayer,
And poured into her soul a flood of light
And then unfolded to her inward sight—
Stern Justice, standing with uplifted hand
And flashing sword, about to smite the land.
She saw a man men named The Bondmen's Friend
Around him gather armies without end;
She saw war's fearful chances bravely faced;
Homes, towns and cities wickedly laid waste;
Gaunt famine reigning, while on every plain
A hundred thousand gallant men lay slain.
At last she saw the dreadful havoc cease;
She heard the proclamation of a peace;
She heard the land rejoice from sea to sea,
And then she knew the slave was free—was free!

   A shock aroused her; 'twas a cruel hand
That rudely pulled her from the salesman's stand;
But as her buyer pushed her through the crowd
She heard a voice—'twas only half aloud,
Though fraught with pathos, anger ill concealed,—
"My God! if ever in a future field

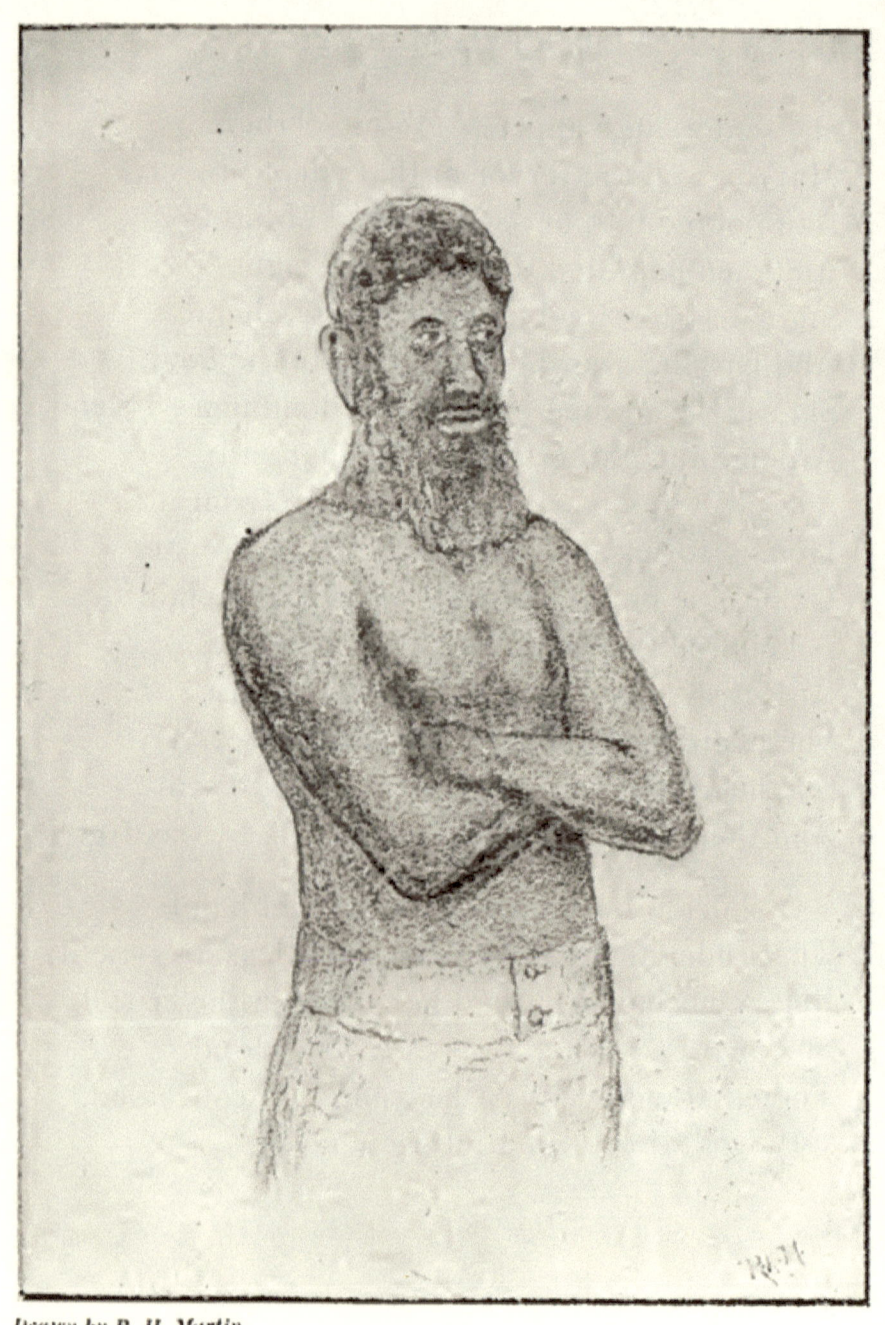

A SPLENDID SAMPLE OF THE RACE ACCURSED.

I have a chance to hit this cursed thing
I'll hit it hard!"
           A strange, prophetic ring
Lingered like music round each fateful word;
A sympathetic chord the woman stirred;
To greet the owner of that God-sent voice,
Destined to make the colored race rejoice,
She let her vision to his face ascend—
Ah! blessed sight! there stood The Bondmen's
      Friend.

CABIN IN WHICH LINCOLN WAS BORN.

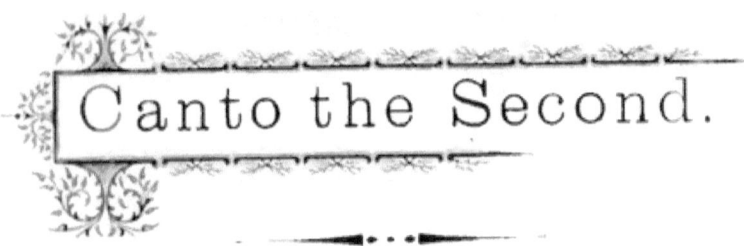

Canto the Second.

Lincoln's Inauguration.

YEARS, heavy laden, slowly rolled away,
Each year unfolding such a dread array
    Of signs portentous that few thinkers failed
To read their meaning.   Then wrong-doers quailed
As in the louring sky, o'erspread with gloom,
There flashed a thirsty sword, the coming doom
Of those oppressors who for greed of gain—
Regardless of the life destroying pain
Their victims felt—enslaved their fellow man,
And thus delayed the grand eternal plan—
God-sent and God-ordained--that this great land
Peerless upon the earth shall always stand;

Shall yield its sceptre unto Truth alone,
While Liberty from her exalted throne
Shall flash the tidings over land and sea
That here, if nowhere else, all men are free.

   Silent and haggard sat The Bondmen's Friend,
As through long vistas—seeming without end—
Of coming woes he sought with eager eyes
Some method God or angels might devise
By which the nation, now on war's dread brink,
Might yet escape, nor be compelled to drink
That bitter draught which all transgressors must
Drain to its dregs and own the fiat just.

   The quest was vain; nor God nor angels deigned
To grant such hope. Then Lincoln's heart was
     pained
That war must be; but since 'twas heaven's decree,
The future ruler bent submissive knee.
"I know," said he, "that liberty is right;
Christ teaches that, and Christ is God, and God's
     my might."

Then were the nation's eyes on Lincoln turned.
And twice ten million hearts for Lincoln burned.
His was the hand they long had wished to find;
His was the counsel, his the strength of mind,
To guide the ardent wills of loyal crowds
To heights of honor up through turmoil's clouds.
Thus, when he left his humble western home;
His goal the nation's fairest, proudest dome;
The woodmen came from forests far and near,
And farmers left their plows to raise a cheer;
The artisans forsook their daily art,
And merchants poured from every bank and mart
To greet with loud huzzas and stirring song
The country's saviour as he rode along.

Oppression's champions heard these gladsome
     songs;
They saw the vast and still increasing throngs
Who based their every hope on Lincoln's word,
And then with hatred deep, by folly stirred,
They laid their dark designs and swore that he—
The man who thought and taught that all are free
By moral laws, the man who dared to say

LINCOLN'S INDIANA HOME.

By permission of S. S. McClure Co.

That state from state can never break away
Should never take the presidential oath.
No; they would hire the dirk and pistol both,
And fill with gold a blood-bespattered hand
To lay in death this menace to the land.

As well might worms defy a tidal wave;
Or dying mortals mock the yawning grave;
Worms, men and nations bow to God's behest;
His will endures, and what he wills is best.

Apprised of danger, Lincoln's friends withdrew
Their modest pageant and their heralds, too.
Their prudence ruled that though he courted light,
His safest route were traversed best at night.
'Twas thus they bore through darkened fields and
    glades,
With prudent speed, their hero and his aids.
And though conspirators were all alert
To do their truest friend a deadly hurt,
Inauguration Day saw Lincoln stand
The most conspicuous man in all the land.

Most fateful hour the nation ever knew!
The far off nations felt its import, too;
And though the gathered crowds would fain be
    glad,
A single glance into that face so sad
All joyful demonstrations soon allayed,
And brilliant statesmen bowed their heads and
    prayed
Prayed that the man who now before them stood,
Their future guide, might be both wise and good;
For though they felt that God's avenging hand
Would shortly fall on this misguided land,
They hoped that virtue at the throne of grace
Might ward the tribulation off a space.

Why was he sad, that man of giant form?
Did his enlightened soul discern the storm
That like a sullen, vengeance-laden cloud—
Destined to humble men, however proud—
Would shortly burst? None but Jehovah knows.
Sad though he was, before both friends and foes
He faltered not to give the world his creed.
Conscious of inborn strength, he saw the need

Of no vainglorious words nor taunting boasts;
His strength was centered on the Lord of Hosts.

"Friends, fellow citizens," said Lincoln then,
"No brotherhood composed of sensate men,
If bound together 'neath one common seal,
Its only bond in life the common weal,
Has ever made provision for its end;
Nor can the wishes of a part transcend
The compact made by all. The bond once made
Must stand for ever. Be not, then, dismayed;
Our Union stands unbroken; still shall be;
Unless the power this day intrusted me
Be taken from me by the spoken will
Of you, my rightful masters. But until
That hour, of which I see no tangent sign,
This simple line of duty shall be mine:
To occupy and hold, wherever found,
The nation's property and then surround
The same with needful strength.—Perchance it
      may
Need more than passive strength.—Now let me say
To you, my fellow countrymen, who chafe and fret.

We are not foes, we meet as brethren yet.
The bonds of love in which we all were trained,
By foolish passions may be somewhat strained;
But break they must not.   Doth not memory yield
The sacred cords that from each battle-field
And patriot grave reach every heart and home,
Where'er on this broad land our brethren roam?
Touched by our better natures, these shall swell
The chorus of the Union till the knell
Of dying nations ushers in the day
When earth and heaven in chaos pass away."

His earnest words burned deep; yea, they did
    more;
They winged their way to every Christian shore,
Where monarchs reigned beneath imperial domes,
And legislators sat in princely homes.
Men skilled in statecraft, stratagem and guile,
Men who could look on war and blandly smile,
By intuition knew that Lincoln stood
Their peer in greatness, that their noble blood
And princely training paled beside the light

Of this rough nobleman whose simple might
And inborn power to rule without deceit
No foe might combat and escape defeat.

Then, with his country's flag around unfurled,
In presence of his God and all the world,
Without intent from duty's path to swerve,
Did Lincoln swear to faithfully preserve,
Protect, defend, as God might give him light,
The Constitution and the people's right.

Thus closed the simple but impressive rite;
And when beneath the shades of restful night
The nation's toilers gathered round the board
The story-tellers drew upon their hoard
Of well selected tales. The children all,
In woodman's hut, in sumptuous, gilded hall,
With eager ears drank in the wondrous tale
Of Lincoln's youth; heard how when young and
    hale
He felled the sturdy pines; that by the light
Of flickering fires that burned the livelong night

He studied hard and filled his mind with lore,
And still he studied to increase the store;
Till, armed at every point, he sallied forth
And championed freedon.   Then the South and
      North,
The East and West soon heard of Lincoln's name,
And knew a giant mind was born to fame.

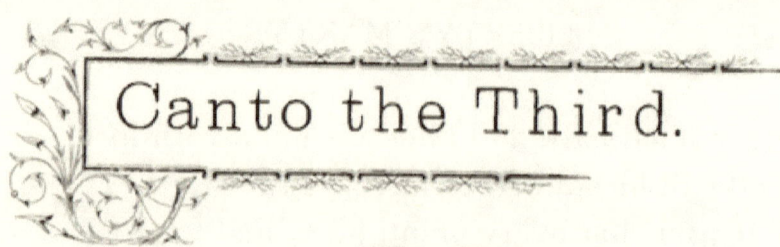

Canto the Third.

Lincoln's First Call For Troops.

GO, ASK a man to buoy a sinking ship;
     To quench a forest fire; or with a grip
        Of human hand to lay a lion low;
Ask him to reap where brave men dare not sow;
To build a lighthouse on a shifting sand;
To gird the round world with an iron band;
These tasks were small, their burden light as air;
Nor could the lot combined in weight compare
With that which Lincoln   not one whit appalled—
Took on his shoulders when his country called.

The point which others aimed at as their goal,
And in the winning threw their heart and soul,
Was but the point where Lincoln's task began.
There, line by line, was God's eternal plan
With steadfast, trusting hand by him unfurled,
Though hostile forces round him stormed and
    swirled.

The Dred-Scott case decision had called forth
A wide-spread storm of wrath throughout the
    North;
John Brown's mad raid had roused the Southern
    ire,
The fancied insult set men's souls afire;
A weakling filled the presidential chair,
Supineness marked his every action there;
Traitors in Congress sat and talked with guile
And stole the nation's arms and wealth the while;
Secession's rumors filled the North with fear,
And wild alarmists turned the public ear
To those who saw in each event a sign
Of this proud nation's ruin and decline.

No piles of bullion had the nation stored;
Her richest merchants held no bursting hoard;
No ships of war patrolled the bounding sea
To guard and keep her ports to commerce free.
Her soldiers all, for ruthless war untrained,
Each at his home an honest living gained.

Already had the rebel yell been heard,
And Anderson at Sumter had been stirred
To promptitude and warlike actions, too;
His energetic spirit saw and knew
That all around intriguers laid their snares,
And schemed to take Fort Sumter unawares.
But still the people of the North forebore
To think a cruel war was nigh; nay, more,
They hoped that wisdom would at once prevail,
And schemes for separation promptly fail.

The day, the fateful day, drew nigh at last
When South to North her gauntlet wildly cast;
When Beauregard his primal shot sent forth
And thrilled the trustful spirits of the North.
That shot, as through the morning air 'twas hurled,

Sent consternation round the Christian world,
Proclaiming, while the nations stood aghast,
That Freedom and Oppression had at last
Unsheathed their swords, that blood must now be
    spilled,
And Freedom's land with Freedom's woes be filled.

   Did Lincoln quail when Sumter's gallant few
From burning walls and threatened death with-
    drew;
When Anderson from out that fort did bring
His country's flag, a torn and tattered thing?
No; for the Northern pulse was burning then;
He calmly sat and with official pen
Called on the states for troops of volunteers
To save the Union.   Quick, with ringing cheers,
Up sprung the nation, ready for the fray,
And organized whole armies in a day.

   The mighty forests, dreary and profound,
Re-echoed with the strange, stentorian sound;
The woodman dropped his axe and sought his gun;
"The Southern foe," said he, "shall fight or run."

The farmer heard it as he wiped his brow,
And straightway in the furrow left his plow;

Went home and charged his wife to pray that harm
Might not befall him; gave the stock and farm
Into her care; then sought the nearest town,
And had his name with volunteers set down.
The merchant called his wife into his store;
Bade her good-bye and through the open door
Threw fervent kisses as he strode away
To face the sabres of the men in gray.
The lawyer left his office and his tomes,
And pastors left their modest, cozy homes,
While men of letters left their desks to fight—
With swords, not pens—for freedom and for right.
The widowed mother called her stalwart boys—
They who had been for years her brightest joys—
Around her chair and bade them every one

Lay down their tools and seek a sword or gun.
"I need you all at home," said she, "and fain
Would keep you, for the parting gives me pain;
But duty to our country says me nay;
A foe to freedom menaces to-day
The torn foundations of our native land;
Then go you forth and join a soldier band.
Fight bravely, boys, and to your flag be true;
Die, rather than disgrace 'the boys in blue.'"

Thus did the patriotic North obey,
And organize whole armies in a day.

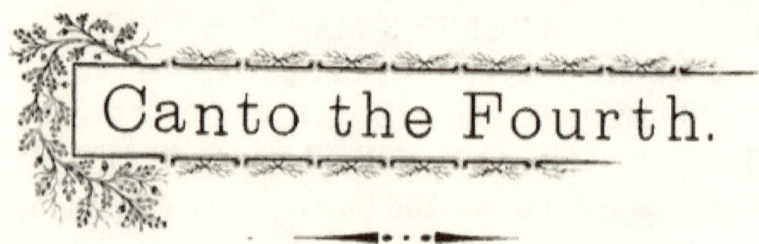

Canto the Fourth.

The Battle of Bull Run.

THE LAMP of night in splendor rode on high,
And fleecy cloudlets graced a placid sky;
The night winds softly touched the forest
trees;
Nature and all her forces seemed at ease;
No jarring note informed the wakeful ear
That aught save peace and harmony was near.

Alas! that nature's most seductive forms
So oft conceal the stealthy march of storms!
That views which seem most restful and serene,
The fiercest wars of passion often screen!

What mean those flickering watch-fires on the
     hill?
Those prostrate soldiers, sleeping now and still?
Those wakeful sentries with their silent tread,
And passwords given with an accent dread?
Why does McDowell stand with eager gaze
And scan the sky for dawning's primal rays?
The tokens all foreshow a deadly fight
When morn's approach shall chase away the night.

     The dawning came at last, and signs of strife
Sprung from earth's bosom into active life.
Two living armies, one in cheery blue
And one in somber gray, appeared in view;
And as morn's brighter rays around them strayed,
A gorgeous scene their moving colors made.

     The soldiers rose and wiped the pearly dew
With zealous care from gun and scabbard, too;
Looked to their powder, ate a hurried meal,
And felt within as only soldiers feel
Who know their only duty is to fight,
And maybe die, to vindicate the right.

Already had the burning July sun
Two thirds his journey toward the noontide run,
When midst a little band of men in gray
A shot was sent, the signal for the fray.
But scarcely had the brunt of war begun
When Hunter fell; his brave career was run.
Then Slocum, too, received his mortal wound,
And soldiers, dead and dying, strewed the ground.
But Hunter's "Blues" soon had the driving hand,
As Sherman joined the fast pursuing band.

Down, down the northern slope of Young's
  Branch ran
McDowell's army, cheering, every man;
The men in gray, too spiritless to cope
With whelming numbers, faced the southern slope
And mounted it with quick, but weary, feet;
Their broken ranks implied no planned retreat.
They reached the summit; there— surprising
  sight!
They found a full brigade in trim to fight
In their defense, a wall of men in gray,
With Jackson in command.

"Away! away!"
Cried Bee to Jackson, see! they beat us back!"
Brave Jackson saw what Bee just then did lack.
"We'll give them bayonets," coolly answered he.
His firm demeanor shamed the flurried Bee;
"Form! Form!" he cried, "See, there, how Jack-
     son stands
Like a stone wall!"   Like thought a thousand
     hands
Gripped with a firmer hold their weapons; then
They turned; they formed, and faced their foes
     like men.
"Stonewall Jackson!" cried the gallant "Grays;"
"Stonewall Jackson!"   Tomes of written praise
Could say no more; its magic pleased the men,
And turned the tide of battle there and then.

   In vain the "Union Boys" with valor strained
Their every nerve to hold what they had gained.
Three times they won—at what a fearful cost!—
The batteries they in weaker moments lost.
In vain they wished for re-enforcements then,
And feigned retreat, then braved the Grays again.

From every side they saw with grim despair,
As dust and smoke begrimed the sultry air
And lengthened shadows told of coming eve,
Their Southern foes some added strength receive.

"Here's Johnston from the vale!" the "Blues"
      at last
In terror cried, and then the die was cast.
The Union soldiers homeward ran a race;
The battle ended, ended in disgrace;
No single soul would heed McDowell's call
To rally once again; their knapsacks all,
Their arms and ammunition strewed the way.
Thus were the "Blues" defeated by the "Gray."

But Lincoln was not vanquished; his reserve
Was still intact. The new recruits might swerve
From duty's path where gleaming swords were
      red,
Where those who fought and those who bravely
      led
Bestrewed a blood-stained field. But, braver man,
The President was ready with his plan.

Disaster on disaster might wring sighs
From his rough nature, tears from his kind eyes;
But from his purpose he could not be moved
Until he had Jehovah's purpose proved.
With mien unruffled Lincoln took his pen,
And called to arms a half a million men.

His timely firmness, like a beacon light
That pierces midnight's gloom and glads the sight,
Cheered and bestirred to greater efforts those
Who, rather than submit to freedom's foes,
Chose war's privations then to promptly brave,
To win their cause or fill a soldier's grave.

Canto the Fifth.

The Merrimac and Monitor.

LONG months of skirmishing each army spent,
Now winning laurels, then in quarters pent;
Despondent one day over vantage lost;
The next day on a wave of triumph tossed;
Each army learned that even leaden hail
'Gainst well trained soldiers was of small avail;
That uninstructed legions, though they stretched
From hill to hill, when skill and courage fetched
A phalanx there, would fall before the foe,
Their strength and numbers melt away like snow.
Both learned the lesson; both for learning paid;

Blood was the price; for many a field displayed
How heroes from the ranks of either side
Had bravely fought and, fighting, bravely died.
To war's mutations thus were all inured,
And each side deemed its own success assured.

  The North had not forgotten that its coasts
Needed protection from the Southern hosts;
The South was mindful that its youthful fleet
Was ill prepared the Northern foe to meet.
Both realized that even on the sea
Neglect might court disaster, which might be
A point from which the conqueror could run –
Elated with a triumph lightly won—
To great and more decisive conquests, till
Experience, blended with increasing skill,
Might force the feebler combatants to yield,
Or fly with fear the last contested field.

  In Hampton Roads, to block the passage way,
Some Northern ships in watchful silence lay.
Yes, they were watchful, for the Southern foe,
With dire intent to strike a fatal blow

At Northern shipping and its forts as well,
Had built a ship designed to ring the knell
Of Northern prestige and of Lincoln's, too,
And crush the hopes of all the Boys in Blue.

Ship, did we call it? 'twas a floating roof
Of heavy iron, shot- and bomb-shell proof.
First of her race was she, and ugly, too,
As any craft that ever loomed in view.

She came and dealt her blows with hellish force;
Her foes replied with shot; but that, of course,
Was powder wasted, for her master laughed
As every shot that struck, both fore and aft,
Glanced swiftly skyward on an aimless quest,
Or plunged beneath in briny mud to rest.
She crushed the Cumberland with horrid ease,
And then, as if the fearful work did please
Her callous master, struck another blow
And sent the Northern war ship down below.
Her sick and wounded found a watery grave;
Nought but her ensign floated o'er the wave.

Straight for the Congress then the monster
    steered;
Elated with success, her gunners cheered;
The ship pursued was promptly run aground;
The Merrimac's commander therefore found
An easy prey at which he blazed with zeal
That made the Congress shiver to her keel.
One half her valiant crew were quickly slain;
The remnant bravely fought, but fought in vain;
The monster's missiles set the ship afire
What greater triumph could the South require!
Could greater glory in a war be earned?
The adversary slain, his war ships burned!

When morning came the Congress was no more;
Her smoking fragments strewed the pebbly shore;
Her living consorts still their ensigns waved,
And dubiously the Southern war ship braved

The Merrimac came down with movement proud;
Her massive beak the wavelets grandly plowed;
The Minnesota seemed an easy prey
To capture and in triumph bear away.

ENGAGEMENT BETWEEN THE MERRIMAC AND THE MONITOR.

But promised glory sometimes proves a dream,
And truly some "things are not what they seem."

The Monitor, a weird, uncanny ship,
Most deftly then let all her moorings slip,
And stood defiant 'gainst that haughty thing
Whose merciless attacks such woe could bring.
The Southern gunners shook their sides and
     laughed;
Called it "a little cheese box on a raft;"
As well they might, although that tiny form
Had faced and braved a fierce Atlantic storm.
Now, proudly confident of latent strength,
Her cool commander placed her dwarf-like length
In trim to fight the ship whose prestige then
Had filled with gloom the minds of Northern men.

The Merrimac commenced the fight with pride;
The Monitor with ponderous shot replied;
But each ship being clad with heavy mail,
The shot rebounded from their sides like hail.
Five times the bigger giant made essay
To run the smaller giant down.   Straightway.

Each time, the smaller giant's guns repelled
The bold attempt, and once, at least, compelled
The bigger ship to run her keel aground;
Then, like a sprite, the stripling danced around,
Seeking and striking each unarmored spot,
And making quarters there intensely hot.

The Merrimac's commander, not yet foiled
Though for a time the sprite his plans had spoiled —
Soon got his ship afloat and steamed straightway
To where the Minnesota waiting lay.
With Southern valor flashing in his eyes,
He swore to take that vessel as a prize,
Or give her with the Cumberland a berth
Where guns and valor are of little worth.

Van Brunt stood ready for the threatened crash;
His broadsides greeted with a stunning flash
The coming vessel. 'Twas of small avail;
For they who lived to tell the stirring tale
Said that her heavy shot, like pebbles, glanced
Harmlessly skyward as the foe advanced.
A shell then pierced the Minnesota's side;

But once again the little demon hied
The bigger one to harrass and to hound,
And forced once more the heavy hull aground.
The Minnesota, thankful it was so,
Rounded and pounded on her stranded foe,
Till he who ruled the primal iron ship
Thought prudence bade him from the combat slip;
With strenuous toil he floated off once more,
And steamed away as if the fight were o'er.

"Stay!"cried the gunner on the lesser ship,
"Before you go I'll try your wings to clip."
Quick after her the Monitor then raced;
The Merrimac in anger turned and faced
The saucy sprite, then rushed with fervid speed
To crush her bold tormentor; but the deed
Brought no results; the well aimed, forceful blow
Struck nought but empty air. The nimble foe,
Armored for such close fighting, forthwith tried
Her weighty shot against her rival's side.
Charge followed charge and each a volley brought,
A quick reply with weight and thunder fraught.

And thus for hours, amid a deafening roar,
A duel raged the like of which before
The world had never seen. The mighty blows
That passed with lightning speed between these
    foes
Stunned and appalled spectators on the land;
The sight, though fearful, was intensely grand.

  To courage, swiftness, skill and strength com-
    bined,
Success in war most often has inclined;
The present conflict no exception proved;
Both ships were damaged, but the bigger moved
First from the combat, and, with sinking stern,
To Norfolk's wharves in gloomy mood did turn.
Dejection clouded her commander's eyes;
He towed not at the stern his promised prize;
He had that day not e'en a war ship burned.
Instead, he had this crushing lesson learned:
Although the South had centered all its skill
In one strong ship, the North, more skillful still,
Had saved its fleet, redeemed its prestige, too,
And given all its hopes a rosy hue.

Throughout the North the cheering tidings
  went,
And forthwith every patriot gave vent
To pent up cheers; and glad, tumultuous notes
Poured, unrestrained and strong, from countless
  throats.
The legislature the inventor praised
Whose skill, unmatched, the nation's hopes had
  raised;
From public platforms and from pulpits, too,
Came eulogies and plaudits not a few.
The press its potent, burning words sent forth
And roused to fervent joy the loyal North.
The people rushed from cities far and near
To gaze delighted and with vision clear
Upon that small, unique, unhandsome thing
Whose prowess made the hills and valleys ring.

Why all this gladness? Why these peals of joy?
The war still raged; the South might yet destroy
The wonder worker; these exultant airs
Again give place to war's perplexing cares!

The President now knew, and knew it well.
The turning point was passed, though none could
    tell
The fierceness of the struggle ere the goal
Would gladden with its light his burdened soul.
He, knowing that Jehovah ever meant
That right shall live unvanquished, smiled content;
His confidence with fervor gladly voiced;
The nation heard it and in sympathy rejoiced.

HANS ANDERSON.
The Last Survivor of the Monitor's Volunteer Crew.

Canto the Sixth.

The Act of Emancipation.

ALTHOUGH the negro long had worn a yoke
And bared his back to many a cruel stroke,
His patient soul divined that he was not
By God forsaken to his hapless lot.
Hope lived within him, pointing with its ray
To some obscured emancipation day.
And yet, commingling with his hopeful song,
Was often heard, "How long, O Lord, how long?"

From husbands who had yielded loving wives
To dark oblivion of their future lives:

From cotton fields where, leaning on his hoe,
The toiler raised no hand to stay the flow
Of welling tears; from many a cabin home
Whence fathers bade inquiring fancy roam
In search of sons and daughters loved too well—
Born, loved and reared for other men to sell;—
From many a mother's heart by anguish torn,
Bereft of all the loved ones she had borne,
Arose incessant plaints against the wrong,
And still they cried, "How long, O Lord, how
      long?"

   From dungeon walls where prisoners shook their
      chains,
And filled the air with weird, religious strains;
From minds beclouded with their thraldom's night;
From mansions where the captives' yoke seemed
      light;
From every Southern dale and cultured plain
The plaintive cry went up with swelling strain.
It rose above the might of ocean's roar
That struck its notes upon the rugged shore;

The clash of warfare in the crimsoned vale
Was drowned beneath this all-important wail;
It gathered volume mid the upland rills,
And swept with grandeur up the wooded hills;
It stayed not in its gracious, heavenward flight
Till in the regions of celestial light —
Attended by a myriad angels there,
An earth-born, earnest, agonizing prayer
From creatures groaning 'neath a cruel rod —
It halted at the very throne of God,
And spread itself in accents pure and strong,
The same refrain, "How long, O Lord, how long?"

An answer from the battlements above
To earth one day descended fraught with love,
Found a responsive chord in Lincoln's heart
And bade him promptly act a steward's part.
To him rare talents had been freely loaned;
For his avenging, souls in waiting groaned;
His was the hand Jehovah had decreed
Should stand between the bondman and his need;
Should strike the shackles from the captive
throngs,
And loose the chorus of ecstatic songs.

Severe reverses, sometimes real defeat,
At times had made the Northern gloom complete.
The Southern armies, therefore, boldly pushed
Their outposts northward, and would soon have
    crushed
With dire defeat the loyal Keystone State;
But loyalty stood armed at every gate;
And even Maryland, th' invader knew,
Did not with favor his intrusion view.

The President, with faith unshaken still,
A trusty weapon held, and held it till
A more auspicious day when victors' songs
Might thrill once more the nation's loyal throngs.
The weapon Lincoln held had been designed
By Him who rules the fates of all mankind;
And though he held it in abeyance now,
The Bondmen's Friend had made a solemn vow—
Thereby to prove the goodness of that hand
Which ruled with chastening then the suffering
    land—
That whensoe'er the Southern army might
From Maryland retreat in driven flight.

He'd crown the blessed victory with a deed
By which the slaves should one and all be freed.

The wished for turn of fortune came at last;
A dreaded crisis had been safely passed;
Antietam's bloody field admonished Lee
That Northern soil, however guileful he
Might be in warfare, still was unsafe ground
For Southern forces; therefore turned he round
And skillfully, but promptly, then withdrew
His menaced army and his outposts, too.

'Twas Lincoln's hour, the climax of his life—
No short-lived semblance of an inward strife
Delayed one moment his responsive pen;
The bravest, kindest, most beloved of men,
The strongest modern friend of humankind
He stood and firmly, but devoutly, signed
The document that made the bondmen free,
Co-heirs with him of heaven-born liberty.

Thus Lincoln, by a bold, decisive stroke,
The galling, hated chains of thraldom broke;
He wiped away a grievous crimson stain

That on his country's record long had lain;
And in the rank of nations foremost placed
A young republic, now no more debased
In sight of Christendom and God because
Of foul oppression sanctioned by its laws.
No blare of trumpets heralded the deed;
For pageantry and pomp he saw no need;
No throng of courtiers did the hour attract;
No ceremonials sanctified the act;
To Lincoln's pure and grandly simple mind
'Twas all sufficient that his God inclined
To look with favor on his steward then
And bless the deed that blessed his fellow men.

The negroes in their lowly cabins heard
The gracious news that all the world had stirred;
And though there yet remained a hundred days
To thraldom's limit, jubilees of praise
Were mingled with each simple, fervent prayer
That rose like incense through the Southern air.
No longer rose that agonized refrain
That once had seemed to smite the heavens in
        vain;

All now had child-like faith and trust in God,
Whose will parental could remove the rod.
Unwavering faith gave wings to those few days,
While hope's effulgent, soul ennobling rays
Broadened and brightened all good things in view,
And made the negro's world seem wholly new.

No pen can faithfully portray the night
That closed the era of the slaver's right
To buy, to brand, or with capricious will
Maltreat his fellow man with studied skill.
The carnal frame is circumscribed on earth;
Its acts, summed up, are oft of little worth;
The mind of man's the fountain of his might;
When that goes free——Ah! who shall track its
    flight?

The aged father sat with moistened eye
And watched the solemn, fateful hours go by;
His gray-haired wife sat near and prayed aloud,
And oft her head in adoration bowed.
Their youngsters—soon their own—refrained from
    sleep,

Glad on that night a holy watch to keep.
Young husbands stood and smiled upon their
    wives
The lights, the joys of all their future lives;
While tender mothers o'er their offspring wept
Hot tears of joy as those dark cherubs slept.

    The fateful moment came, the midnight sound,
And straightway, with a glad, ecstatic bound,
Praise and loud hallelujahs filled the air;
Tears, holy tears of joy, fell everywhere.
The aged pilgrim clasped his tottering wife —
His own at last, though near the end of life—
And mingled praises with her earnest prayers
That few henceforth might be their earthly cares;
The youthful husband took a fresh embrace
Of his young wife, and on her upturned face
Wept tears of rapture. Both were happy then;
They knelt and prayed, then wept with joy again.
Each happy mother praised the Lord aloud
And waked a chorus from the sable crowd
Of youngsters scampering o'er the cabin floor,
Who wondered wherefore all this glad uproar.

Joy, unrestrained, burst forth in varied song;
From south to north its volume rolled along;
Fom east to west it sped with swelling sound;
It stayed not till it roved the world around;
And still it echoes God's benign decree,
Which Lincoln penned, that here all men are free.

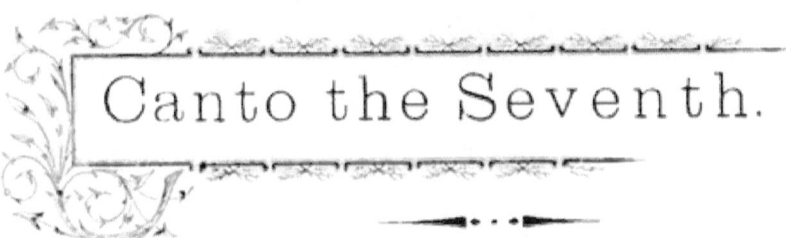

Canto the Seventh.

The Last Year of the War.

THE martial notes that struck each Southern
hill
Proclaimed the crimson war-stream flowing
still;
Its sinuous progress o'er the charred expanse
Of vales once verdant marked the stern advance
Of conquering legions. They were "men in blue,"
Who fought for freedom and the Union, too.

The bravely stubborn men who wore the gray
Found their resources dwindling day by day,

Their utmost skill with greater skill attacked,
Their forts dismantled and their cities sacked.
Both armies wished to check the loss of life;
Both bravely fought to end the bloody strife;
But every soldier in his soldier foe—
On march triumphant or in dust laid low—
Discerned a patriot, both true and brave,
Who gave his life his country's life to save.

The march of war seemed but a weary plod,
Men called for haste; but still the mills of God
Ground slowly, though they ground exceeding
      small;
Nor could a mortal's haste God's plan forestall.

Haste genders rashness; rashness often ends
In dire disaster; but the man who blends
A prudent patience with a knowledge when
To strike may fight and live to fight again.
Such men in warfare are great men indeed;
And such were Grant and Sherman. They agreed
To try what each, eschewing haste, could do
By "hammering" at the South the summer through.

They planned to harrass with persistent skill,
To give no rest, no breathing times, until
The final blow should tell of war's surcease
And sound the keynote of the wished-for peace.

Their plans matured, each general went his way
To plague forthwith the South from day to day.
Grant marched into the Wilderness and there
Harrassed the foe with might and zealous care.
His object was on Richmond to advance;
But Lee's troops led him many a weary dance;
And many a fierce engagement there was fought,
And every victory was dearly bought.
Yet Grant was stubborn, dogged, brave and true;
And though 'tis said ten thousand "men in blue"
Fell in one fight, he dreamed not of retreat;
His was a mood that never knew defeat.

Meanwhile, from Chattanooga Sherman moved
Upon Atlanta. There the soldier proved
That, though a conqueror, he was still inspired
With human kindness; for although he fired
The mills and foundries with relentless hand

He let the dwellings and the churches stand.
Then marched he from Atlanta to the sea;
Rain from the heavens and bullet-rain from Lee
Stayed not his march.   His troops were now
        inured
To war's mischances, and all ills endured
With resignation.   E'en the cheerful song
Lightened their footsteps as they tramped along.
Each day the war's last battle nearer seemed;
Each night of home scenes many a soldier
        dreamed.

  At last! At last! the cruel war was o'er;
Right was triumphant; Freedom, battle sore,
Was Freedom still; unvanquished, yet alert.
By mercy swayed, to heal her foeman's hurt.
Stayed was war's havoc; stayed, the waste of life;
All arms were stacked; the purpose of the strife
Forgotten in the eagerness of men
To tie the bonds of brotherhood again.

  Where then was Lincoln, he whose anxious eye
Had watched the troublous months and years go
        by?

Where was the man who skillfully had steered
The ship of state through dangers all else feared;
Whose courage saved the Union and removed
The bane that had almost its ruin proved?
Not as a judge sat he condemning those
To punishment who were his vanquished foes;
Not on a throne sat he with pomp to wait
The nation's plaudits of the good and great;
Nor in a chariot rode he that all eyes
Might see his glory like a halo rise.

In Richmond's streets the Bondmen's Friend
        was found;
A thousand negroes hemmed his path around;
Each vied with each to greet with honest smile
The nation's head, and bless his name the while.
Each earnest preacher, with stentorian voice,
Called on his flock to thank God and rejoice
That they had been permitted thus to see
The man whose greatness made the lowly free.
Then every singer in that happy throng
Wove Lincoln's name in his exultant song:

And, as their plaudits fell on Lincoln's ear,
His smile was brightened by a glistening tear;
Their joy was all his grateful soul could crave;
The simple scene more satisfaction gave
Than perorations which the crowds commend,
Or lofty strophes by a poet penned.

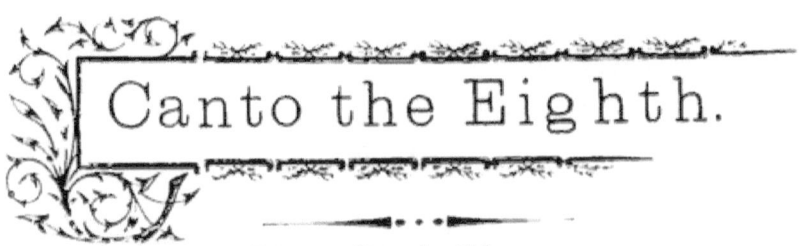

Canto the Eighth.

The Final Blow.

MEN FELT relieved and hopeful that at last
    Their country's darkest period had been
        passed;
That peaceful homes no more by hostile hordes
Should be destroyed; that guns and blood-red
    swords
Henceforth should hang exempt from war's dark
    crimes—
Mementoes only of those troublous times.
Abroad, the friends of freedom all rejoiced;
At home, the nation's joy had scarce been voiced.
The cause for joy, 'tis true, was full and grand;
It brightened every hamlet in the land;

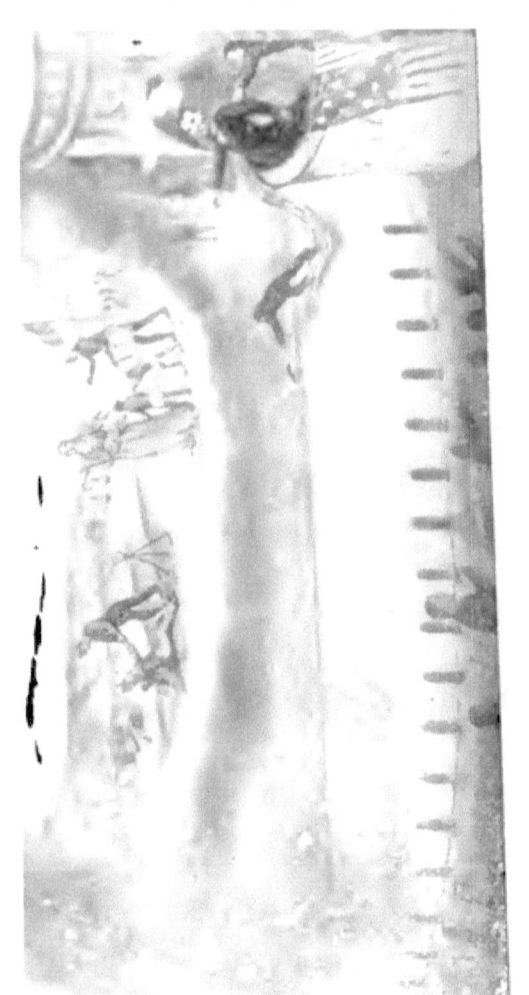

Drawn by *Antoinette Wall.*

THE FINAL BLOW.—BOOTH'S BULLET FINDS ITS AIM.

But 'twas a joy that blended oft with grief
For Southern woes that called for prompt relief.

One evil sign told yet of coming ill—
The sword of Justice flashed in anger still.
Men saw it not; but heaven's astonished throngs
Paused ere they struck the notes of joyful songs;
Then swiftly gathered round the vengeful form,
And thus essayed to turn the threatened storm:

"Ho! Justice, sheathe thy weary weapon now;
Canst thou not see how many millions bow
In gratitude to God that all seems o'er?
Why dash their hopes? Why rend the healing
    sore?
Thy ruthless sword with blood has long been wet;
Stay, stay thy hand!" But Justice cried "Not yet."

"Ho! Justice, gaze upon the crimsoned vales;
See bleaching bones define the conquerors' trails;
See desolation where sleek herds once grazed;
And homes, once happy, now in ashes razed.
List to the tones of overwhelming grief
Bursting from hearts doomed ne'er to know relief;

List to the widows mourning husbands dead;
To mothers wailing o'er the spirits fled;
See other nations haste to sympathize
With this one's woes; then surely from the skies
Should grace descend. Oh! Justice, stay thy hand,
And smite no more the contrite, suffering land.
Four years of war have surely paid its debt."
But Justice, still unmoved, replied "Not yet."

Amid the glad pulsations of a crowd,
Before the shrine of recreation bowed;
With war's dread tidings now no more depressed,
The mind of Lincoln sought its needed rest.
His honest soul had not divined that hate —
The last foul spark—might there in ambush wait.
But so it was; the tragic moment came —
A sharp report!—Booth's bullet found its aim,
And Lincoln fell. Oh! there was horror then
And blank despair! The surging waves of men
Could scarce command the words with which to
        swear—
By highest heaven—that he whose form lay there
Should be avenged. The nation felt the wound;

And every heart, the startled country round,
Bled with fierce anguish, deep, but unconcealed—
Anguish that to the world its throes revealed.
Great God! what passions stirred the masses then!
"Revenge! Revenge!" ten thousand cried again—
A thousand lives could not for this atone!—
The life of Lincoln, brilliant and alone,
Was virtue, freedom, love for all mankind—
Three blessings in the nation's head combined.

But o'er the masses thus with anger swayed
A voice with power in earnest accents strayed—
"God reigns above; our nation liveth still!"
The people heard, then bowed to heaven's will.
Thus was the nation's fiercest trial past,
And Justice sheathed her crimson sword at last.

Did Lincoln die? Did his magnific mind
Cease work because the gaze of humankind
No longer saw life's motions in the frame
That erst had housed his soul and borne a name?
No. Such a mind lives on, for ever lives,
And of its plenitude rich treasure gives

To nations seeking heaven's benignant light —
His very name dispels oppression's night.
Through him the world has learned, is learning
    still,
The might of right, backed by a strong man's
    will.
And through unnumbered years that yet may roll
Ere Freedom shall o'er every vale and knoll
Of this tumultuous earth her sceptre sway,
The mind of Lincoln will not rest nor stay;
But live to conquer, while a stainless fame
Shall daily add new lustre to his name.

Brothers, All.

FROM my home in youth I wandered
　Far and wide o'er scenes terrestrial;
　Saw the races dark and swarthy,
And the yellow-faced Celestial;
Stunted Esquimaux and Red Men
Scorned by pale-faced men and others;
But, despite contempt and scorning,
All I recognized as brothers.

'Neath the equatorial splendor
Of the sun's effulgent beaming;
Where the plains are ever baking
And the broad lagoons are steaming;
Where the atmosphere malarial
Slays the Englishman and others—
There the black and stalwart negroes
Dwell, and they are all my brothers.

Deep amid the forest tangle,
Where the night winds answer, moaning
To the howling of the jackal
And the bleeding victim's groaning—
There I found the man whom some say
Has no conscience crime can smother;
Yet in him, amidst his baseness,
Lo! I recognized a brother.

Where the isles of ocean glisten
Like the gems on heaven's portals;
And the God-sent bread-fruit ripens—
Food for throngs of favored mortals—
Where in days gone by the wild men
Plundered, slew and ate each other;
Though degenerated sadly,
Still I recognized a brother.

Back again among the alleys,
Slums and by-ways of the city,
Where the air is thick with curses;
Where the dulcet tones of pity

Seldom reach the ears of children
Born of creatures miscalled mothers—
There I found—polluted, loathsome,—
Fallen sisters, sinful brothers.

O, ye dreamers, learned prophets,
Orators and bold reformers,
Gabbling politicians, authors,
Zealots, priests and pulpit stormers!—
Earth will never be an Eden
Till the claims and rights of others—
Black men, white men, red or yellow—
Are respected as our brothers'.

Only a Rose.

"ONLY a rose," said a heedless girl,
  As it fell from her breast to the dusty street;
  It was soon forgotten mid hurry and whirl
And the tramp of a thousand busy feet.
But a shoeless lad had espied the flow'r
And carried it off as a wondrous prize;
It cheered a sick brother through many an hour,
And brightened his languishing, dying eyes.

  Only a rose; but 'twas piously laid
With tenderest care on a verdureless grave;
And its petals a halo of sweetness made
Like that which the bowers of Eden gave;
And it gladdened the heart of that orphan boy
As he laid it down on that mound to rest;
For he said "It will heighten my brother's joy
To see me fulfilling his last request."

We're Homeward Bound.

ONCE restless Fancy left her home,
  Across the wide, wide world to roam;
  And wandering where so often rest
The ships asleep on Ocean's breast,
She hovered near a vessel fair,
Where, poised upon the midnight air,
Amid the stilness, else profound,
She heard a voice "We're homeward bound."

  She saw that vessel tempest driven,
Her bulwarks broke, her topsails riven;
Her laboring hull and battered form
A target for the cruel storm;
She saw the wild waves breaking o'er
Her decks where all was peace before;
But still the hope inspiring sound
Broke through the storm "We're homeward
    bound."

She saw that graceful vessel glide—
Befriended by both wind and tide·—
Into a harbor's safe retreat
Where long lost vessels daily meet;
And though upon her damaged form
She bore the marks of many a storm,
Her crew still sang with cheering sound
The glad refrain "We're homeward bound."

She saw a child of humble birth
Launch out upon this stormy earth;
And mid the waves and shoals of life,
Mid rocks of grief and whirls of strife,
Long time he sought what humankind
So often seek but seldom find.
At last a guiding hand he found
On which was writ "We're homeward bound."

That guiding hand he followed long,
When pains were sharp and grief was strong;
When that grim monster Death bereaved,
With meekness he the blow received;

Or when misfortune tore away
The gains he toiled for day by day,
Above each woe would still resound
The cheering lay "We're homeward bound."

She saw the man, grown old and gray,
Walk warily life's lonesome way;
But though his faltering gait betrayed
The inroads fell disease had made;
Though rapid strides he dared not try,
A ray of hope lit up his eye
And cheered him o'er the toilsome ground,
As still he read "We're homeward bound."

And when at length the final storm
Laid low his fragile, tottering form;
When Death, to end his earthly race,
Stood gaunt before the old man's face;
The legend, still with comfort fraught,
To sinking nature solace brought—
His last wish this: "Above my mound
This motto write, 'We're homeward bound.'"

Side by Side.

THEY were sitting side by side in life's morning
    bright and fair;
He was ruddy, strong and healthy; she pos-
    sessed a beauty rare;
They were only little children; yet their converse
    was of love.
And their simple-worded promises were registered
    above.

They were learning side by side, under teachers
    grave and wise;
And they drank from founts of knowledge that
    for youthful learners rise;
And his help was freely given with such tender-
    ness and grace
That her gratitude was ever beaming through her
    lovely face.

They were playing side by side, and his ever
    watchful eye,
Like a loving guardian angel, was for ever hover-
    ing nigh;
They were 'mid the snares of childhood, but his
    arm so young and strong
Saved her fair and fragile figure from impending
    harm and wrong.

They were walking side by side when their school
    days all had flown;
When the rose of early manhood in his healthful
    face had blown;
When her beauty, like a fragrance, lured him
    often to her side,
And again they vowed that never aught but death
    should part them wide.

They were standing side by side—'twas the long
    sought hour of bliss—
When the ritual was concluded, and the sacred,
    honest kiss

Was bestowed with welcome fervor, as the newly
    wedded wife,
Leaning on his manly vigor, launched upon the
    sea of life.

They were fighting side by side in life's battle,
    roar and din,
In the struggle for existence, midst the whirls of
    strife and sin;
But they bravely faced each danger, though they
    never sought a foe,
And they shared the victors' laurels when the
    almond flow's did blow.

They were resting side by side in their cottage
    old and gray;
Waiting, waiting, calmly waiting for the separa-
    tion day.
Still the unextinguished fires of their ancient love
    burned high;
Though the ears of both were heavy, and a cloud
    bedimmed each eye.

They are lying side by side in the grave-yard
'neath the sod,
Where they rest from all their labors till the
mighty trump of God
Shall recall to forms of beauty souls that from
our vision glide,
And replace the loving spirits in his kingdom
side by side.

Music.

I STOOD where Babylonia's streams
  Glide with funereal pace
    And melancholy grace
Beneath the sheen of Luna's playful beams.

Luxuriant willows graced the scene,
  Enhancing evening's charms
    And banishing alarms;
For Riot dared not come where Peace was
  queen.

The north wind moaned a plaintive wail,
  And Echo scarcely heard
    The love songs of that bird
Whose trilling oft pervades the sleeping vale.

A band of harpers, bending low
  Each grief worn, anxious face,
    Approached the hallowed place
With drooping gait and footsteps sad and
  slow.

There, underneath the willows' shade,
  They struck a mournful lay
  That drove all joys away—
Then Sorrow came and lamentation made.

My peace was gone; gone was my joy;
  Nor could they soothe again
  The heart they smote with pain—
Their cords vibrated only to destroy.

I stood where Riot reigned supreme;
  Where all the songs of mirth
  That ever yet had birth
Were blended like the figures in a dream.

Fantastic airs and swelling notes·
  Of wild, hilarious lays,
  Joy, rapture, love and praise
Poured, unmelodious, from a myriad throats.

The drum, the harp, the trembling lyre,
  The sweetly plaintive lute,
  The breathing, vocal flute,
Conspired to fill my soul with fierce desire.

But from them all I turned aside—
    As cloudlets, light and rare,
    Melt in the summer air,
Those evanescent pleasures paled and died.

I stood beneath a dome profound,
    Where all the builder's will
    Was patent in the skill
Displayed to catch and heighten every
    sound.

An organist was there whose hands
    Seemed touched with heaven's fire,
    So high did he aspire
    As if his life's desire
Was to out-measure heaven's seraphic
    bands,

Above the earth my soul he bore
    Into a wide abyss
    Of wild, ecstatic bliss,—
    Joy followed swelling joy;
    Raptures without alloy

Rose, bearing me along
On tempest whirls of song
Beyond—aye, far beyond—life's tuneless
    roar.

Alas! one harsh, false note he played,
    And back upon the world
    My wounded soul was hurled,
Like soaring dove struck by the zigzag
    blade.

I stood where none but dreamers stand,
    And heard this mighty sphere
    Roll out, year after year,
Its own majestic tones from sea and land.

Each living creature raised its voice
    In concert as the sun
    His blithesome task begun,
And bade each other tunefully rejoice.

The forest trees, a stately band,
    Like minstrels stood and played;
    They caught each breeze that strayed,
Transforming every breath to sweetness
    grand.

Each little brook essayed a song;
    Each wavelet sung its lay;
    While through the ceaseless day
Niagara's voice was musical and strong.

The ocean roared against the main;
    A thousand caves replied;
    Their echoes swelled and died.
And rolling thunders toned a grand refrain.

Though all else pleased, I could not close
    My still attentive ear
    To tones of pain and fear—
Soul piercing tones that told of earthly woes.

I stood where legions of redeemed,
    From every tribe and clime,
    In every age and time,
Through heaven's open gate have gladly
    streamed.

One great ambition swayed me then;
    It promised perfect bliss,—
    Ah! did I seek amiss?—
To learn and bring heaven's music down to
    men.

It could not be; a seraph bright,
   Benevolent and kind,
   My ardent wish divined,
And sped to shut all heaven from my sight.

Yet in my visions, passing fair,
   He came with goodness filled,
   And through my soul instilled
This new conception of the music there:

In yon blest realm, where love doth dwell,
   No dubious words can vex,
   Nor foreign tongues perplex—
Music is heaven's language;—learn it well.

The Genuine Man.

IN A DREAM I was seeking a genuine man,
  And a man with a pure, lofty aim;
    So I sailed to the east and I rode to the west,
Till my journeyings brought me some fame—
From the frost of the north to the ice of the south,
Over every dominion between;
But the bright, beaming face of a genuine man
Was a gem that but seldom was seen.

All the monarchs of earth in their regal attire
Passed beneath my inquisitive gaze;
And their splendor and pomp were a sight to
      behold,
For bedazzling were royalty's rays;
But the pageantry faded, the lustre all died,
When the blaze of their presence had passed,
And I loitered in vain on their track to discern
If a perfume their lifetimes had cast.

Then the grandees came on with a proud,
    haughty mien
And their tall genealogical trees,
While the servitors fawningly walked in their
    train,
Or they grovelled the lordlings to please.
Amid sporting and feasting these lived out their
    day,
And they passed from life's changeable scene;
But the names that still shone when the dust
    claimed its own
Were but feeble and distant between.

Then a concourse I saw, and each one had a
    tongue
That was oiled when the owner thought meet;
And for those who are easily flattered or gulled
They had always a wonderful treat.
By their cozening, lying and promising much
They secured the high seats they desired,
Where a few of them shone; but alas! for their
    light,--
But a moment it blazed, then expired.

From my view point so high, then, perforce, I came
    down.
And I mixed with the general crowd,
With the wise and the subtle, the sordid, the
    throng
Who for ages to Mammon have bowed;
And I found here and there—but alas! they were
    scarce —
On the sand of life's wave beaten shore,
The deep footprints of those who to benefit men
Have devoted time, talents and store.

They have lived with an aim that they never
    forgot —
E'en amid their own seasons of woe;
And that aim was to brighten the dark spots of
    life,
And to show where the brighter ones glow;
To proclaim to their kind that each man has a
    place
That no man but himself can well fill;
And that duty neglected, whate'er the excuse,
To the whole world can bring nought but ill.

Then the genuine man is a man whom the world,
Be it never so wicked, will own
Has a claim to be honored, respected and loved,
And to occupy memory's throne;
And his name upon history's pages shall shine
Like a gem amid pebbles or clay,
And the record of deeds he accomplished in life
Be a chart to show millions their way.

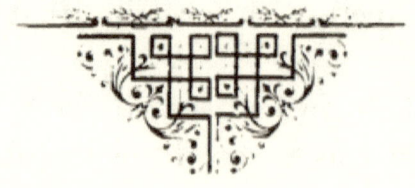

A Sigh from the City.

WHERE the crystal streamlet floweth:
    Where the fragrant briar groweth,
    And the south wind gently bloweth,
        I would gladly stray;
Where the sun his glory lendeth
To the verdant bough that bendeth
O'er the stream that onward tendeth—
        Bask the hours away.

There. beneath a tree reclining—
Heaven and earth around me shining—
Gazing on the silver lining
        Of each passing cloud;
Lost in blissful admiration:
O the pleasing situation!
Brief. but blessed separation
        From the sordid crowd!

A SIGH FROM THE CITY.

There the bee industrious singeth,
All day long her voyage wingeth
O'er the region whence she bringeth
   Earth's ambrosial food;
There the merry cricket danceth;
There the fleet-winged swallow glanceth
Midst the throng whose hum enhanceth
   Nature's happy mood.

From the scenes arousing pity;
From the dreary, smoky city,
With its unmelodious ditty,
   Gladly would I stray;
Where the joys of earth are dearer;
Where the views of heaven are clearer,
And the bliss of heaven seems nearer,
   Bask the hours away.

The Wide, Wide Sea.

O THERE'S nought like a trip on the wide,
wide sea
Where the sea-birds rove and the winds are
free;
Where the wavelets dance o'er the boundless view,
And the sunshine heightens their beauteous blue;
Where the porpoise gambols and turtles sleep
In the ceaseless plash of the sleepless deep;
Where revel the hugest forms that be—
Then O for a trip on the wide, wide sea!

When the turmoils of life, like a thorny load,
Bewilder me, harrass me, worry and goad;
When the toiling limbs and the active brain,
Or the body distressed by wasting pain,
Require a rest and a bracing air,
Let me sail on thy bosom, thou sea so fair:
For there's life in thy fragrance, and health for me;
Then O for a trip on the wide, wide sea!

The Lovers' Good Night.

WE STOOD at the end of the rustic street
Where the village youngsters nightly meet;
But the village youngsters were all abed—
And the moon, from the canopy overhead,
Looked down on a pleasing sight;
For her hand was clasped in a hand of mine,
And her eyes with the starting tears did shine,
And a sigh escaped her little frame;
It came unbidden, but still it came,
When one of us said "Good night."

I will not say which of us said the word;
But the other one seemed to have never heard;
For our hands lost not their impulsive hold——
And the stars in their nightly courses rolled
Like diamonds rare and bright;
While the dew came down on the way-side grass;
And the lightsome hours did lightly pass;

But I still held her hand, and she held mine—
Two hours before had the clock struck nine;
    We knew it and said "Good night."

    But hands do not always obey the will;
She tightened her grasp and I held her still;
The morrow would come, and the briny tide
With its ruthless billows would us divide;
    And years, in their lazy flight,
Might deaden the love that was now aflame—
Such thoughts, unbidden, unwelcomed, came—
The birds from their warbling mates might fly;
Our love for each other should never die;
    We promised, and said "Good night."

    But still my fingers were unreleased;
The strength of my hold on hers increased;
The language of love, like a murmuring rill,
Flowed softly and smoothly on until
    The moon refused us her light;
A policeman passed on his nightly tour,
And the village clock struck the midnight hour,

THE LOVERS' GOOD NIGHT.

As a chilling breeze, like a peri's sigh,
From the gorse clad hills came sweeping by —
    We shivered and said "Good night."

  As if by elves' enchantments chained,
Our hands in that mystic grasp remained;
Not e'en the chilling midnight breeze,
Nor health's unbending, stern decrees
    Could shorten our love's delight;
But time stays not for lovers' prayers;
The morrow's woes, the morrow's cares
Must each be met—we knew it well—
One awful wrench!--we broke the spell;
    We kissed, and we said "Good night."

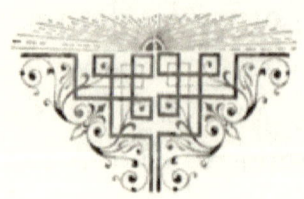

www.ingramcontent.com/pod-product-compliance
Lightning Source LLC
Chambersburg PA
CBHW022148020726
47496CB00008B/2622